How Colorado Became the Centennial State

How Colorado Became the Centennial State

NOW YOU  KNOW MORE

Barbara Taylor

Filter Press, LLC
www.FilterPressBooks.com

How Colorado Became the Centennial State
Copyright © 2025 by Barbara Taylor
First edition

All rights reserved. Except for brief passages quoted in newspapers, magazines, radio or television reviews, podcasts, and electronic media, no part of this book may be reproduced in any form or by any means, electronic or mechanical, without permission in writing from the publisher.

This work is the work of human creativity and research, crafted without the use of generative AI in its writing. Any use of this publication to train generative artificial intelligence is expressly prohibited.

ISBN: (Paperback): 978-0-86541-272-9
ISBN: (eBook): 978-0-86541-273-6
Library of Congress Control Number: 2025943832
Cover design: Jordan Ellender
Cover images: Map of Colorado Territory, 1866, drawn by Fredrick J. Elbert; 38-star US flag courtesy of Jeff R. Bridgman Antiques, Inc., www.JeffBridgman.com

Filter Press, LLC
Westcliffe, Colorado
www.FilterPressBooks.com
Info@FilterPressBooks.com

For Coloradans:
Happy Birthday, Colorado

& for Julie, who always knows and loves
a great story

Contents

1 Colorado Statehood 1

2 Gold 3

3 Setting the Stage 9

4 1859—Auraria Convention 13

5 1860 to 1861—Civil War Stalls Statehood 19

6 1862 to 1864—Turbulent Politics 25

7 1865—Statehood Skeptics 29

8 1866 and 1867—Vetoes 36

9 1868 to 1875—Almost a State 39

10 1876—Statehood at Last 45

11 The Centennial State 50

Timeline 55

New Words and Terms 59

Sources 64

Congregate a hundred Americans any where beyond the settlements, and they immediately lay out a city, frame a State Constitution, and apply for admission into the Union, while twenty-five of them become candidates for the United States Senate.

-Albert D. Richardson, *Our New States and Territories, Being Notes of a Recent Tour of Observation through Colorado, Utah, Nevada, Oregon, Montana, Washington Territory and California,* 1866

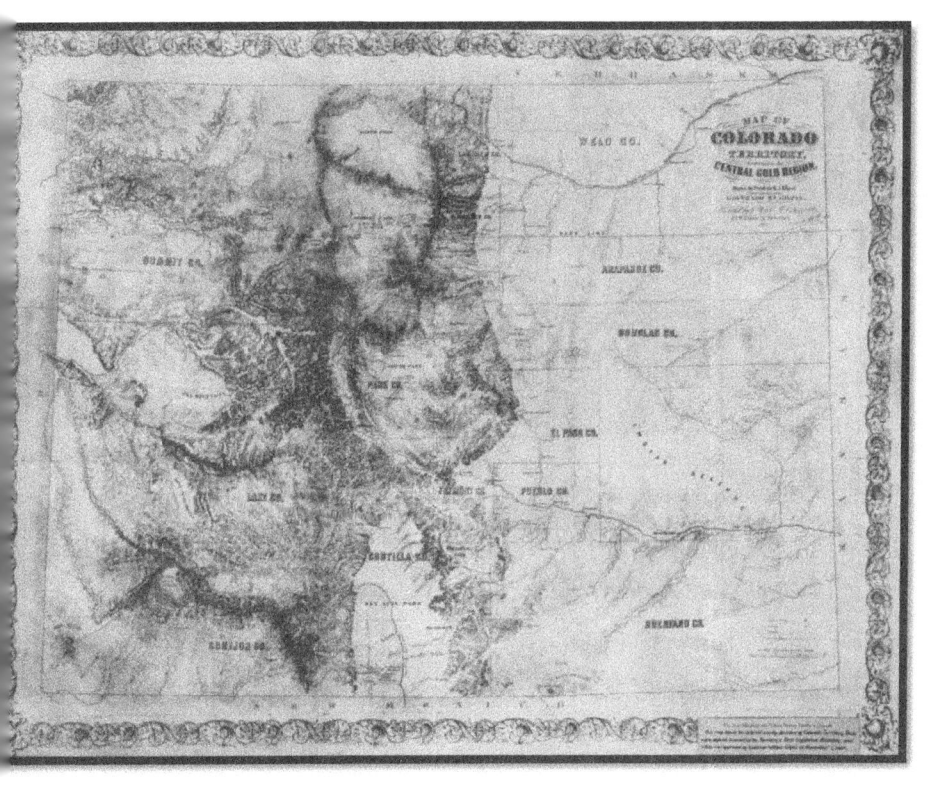

Map of the Colorado Territory, 1861, drawn by Frederick J. Ebert

1 Colorado Statehood

The first issue of *The Rocky Mountain News* included an article about a pioneers' meeting on April 11, 1859, in "Uncle" Dick Wootton's Auraria gambling saloon. The men met to discuss their goal of forming a new state. The meeting took place less than a year after discoveries by the William Green Russell party sparked the **Pikes Peak gold rush.**

Miners had arrived in the region and begun to actively **prospect** on land granted to Native Americans by **peace treaties.** Nonetheless, this group of men living in Auraria and Denver City, communities on either side of Cherry Creek near the confluence of the South Platte River, were already thinking about statehood.

During the next seventeen years, **slavery**, the **Civil War**, turbulent and shifting **politics**, conflicts between settlers and **Native American** tribes, calls for Black male and women's **suffrage**, and land ownership questions would all play a role in delaying and defining Colorado's statehood.

Finally, on August 1, 1876, one hundred years after the signing of the Declaration of Independence, President Ulysses S. Grant issued a **proclamation** declaring the admission of Colorado into the Union as the thirty-eighth state. It was the only state admitted that year and was nicknamed the **Centennial** State.

This is the history behind Colorado's long and twisted road to statehood.

A thirty-eight-star American flag used to honor Colorado as the Centennial State
Courtesy of Jeff R. Bridgman Antiques, Inc., www.JeffBridgman.com

2 Gold

Rumors about gold discoveries in Colorado's Rocky Mountains date to the sixteenth century when Spanish **explorers** found gold and silver in Central and South America. Explorers began searching the American Southwest, hoping to find **Indigenous people** who knew the location of more gold.

In an 1806–1807 **expedition**, explorer Zebulon Pike and his men left Fort Bellefontaine near St. Louis. After crossing the Great Plains, they followed the Arkansas River into present-day Colorado. When they reached the mountains, Pike's party attempted to climb the peak that would later carry his name (Pikes Peak) but failed to reach the summit. Continuing along the Arkansas River, the explorers entered South Park, stumbled upon the Royal Gorge, and crossed over the Sangre de Cristo Mountains into the San Luis Valley.

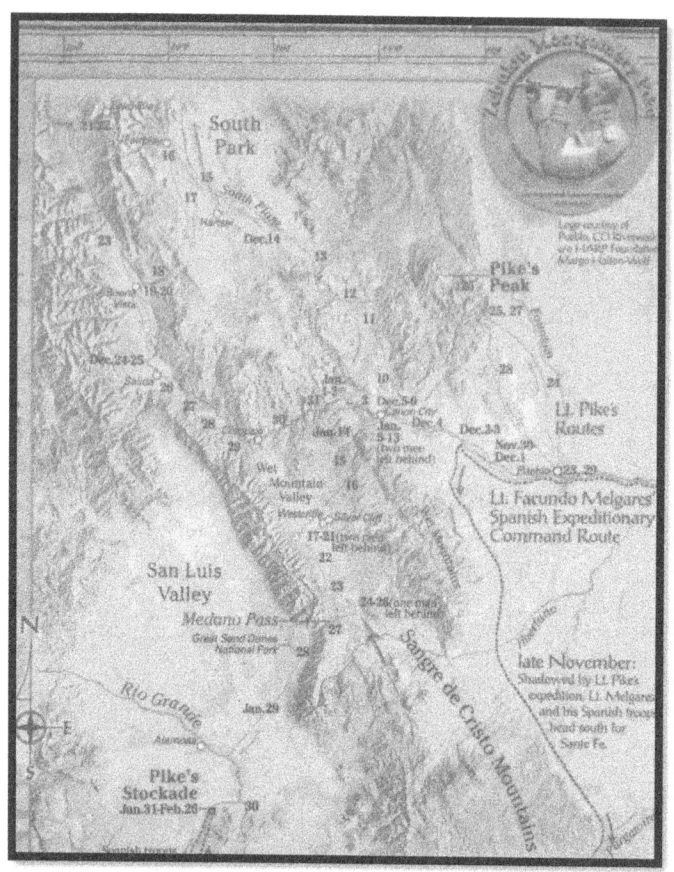

Map showing Pike's route through Colorado
Courtesy of the Pueblo Riverwalk

At the time of Pike's expedition, Spain had claimed all **territory** south of the Arkansas River. Because Pike was trespassing on Spanish land, he was arrested and taken to Santa Fe, where he met trapper James Purcell. Purcell told Pike that he had found gold in the headwaters of the Platte River.

During the early 1800s, trappers and explorers

made small gold discoveries in the Rocky Mountains. Then, in the summer of 1858, the Russell brothers and their party discovered **placer gold** in Little Dry Creek in present-day Englewood.

Their discovery started the Pikes Peak gold rush.

Before the Pikes Peak gold rush, the plains and mountains that would eventually become Colorado were home to Native Americans, **Hispano** settlers in the south, and a few trappers and explorers. Approximately fifty-one Native American tribes called the plains and mountains of Colorado home. In the thirty years following the Pikes Peak gold rush, almost all these Native American tribes were forcibly removed from their homelands.

A Pikes Peaker crossing the plains, drawn by Albert Bierstadt, *Harper's Weekly*, August 13, 1859

Ernest House Jr., a member of the Ute Mountain Ute Tribe, described this removal in a 2023 Colorado Public Radio interview. He said, tribes were removed "by treaty or by gunpoint."

Gold gets the glory, but several other factors were important in enticing settlers to the West. Both the 1857 **economic downturn** in the East and several important Native American treaties, including the **Fort Laramie Treaty of 1851** and the **Fort Atkinson Treaty of 1853**, helped encourage the rush. These treaties aimed to establish peace and to ensure safe passage for settlers traveling through tribal lands.

Perceptions of a safer West, where one could easily find riches, encouraged migrants from the East to seek their fortune in the Rocky Mountains.

In January 1859, George Jackson discovered gold near present-day Idaho Springs. Around the same time, John Gregory discovered gold near Black Hawk. These discoveries added to the excitement and the belief that gold was easy to find. The race to the Rockies was on.

By the end of 1859, the Pikes Peak gold rush had drawn approximately a hundred thousand individuals, although the number who arrived and stayed is estimated at closer to forty thousand. Pioneers often arrived, spent a couple of months searching for gold, and then left poorer than

Gold

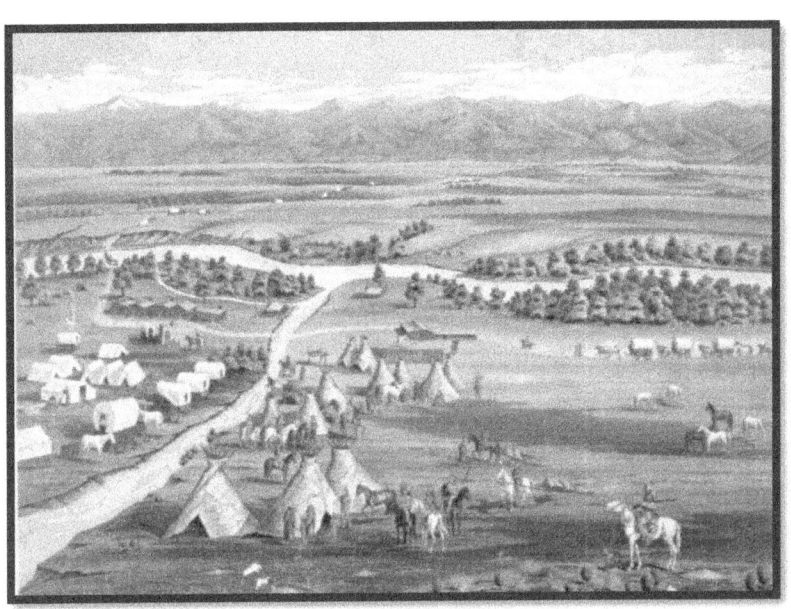

Denver City and Auraria in 1859. These settlements were on either side of Cherry Creek, near its confluence with the South Platte River.
Courtesy of the Library of Congress, 3B49610, Collier & Cleveland Litho Co.

they'd come. These miners were called "go backers" by those who stayed.

Auraria, Denver City, Mountain City, Central City, Golden, Idaho Springs, and other towns formed in the mountains and along the **Front Range**. With these towns and Colorado's increased **population** came the need for rules and government.

Know More
States and Territories

In 1787, eleven years after the United States declared independence from Great Britain, Delaware was the first of the thirteen original colonies to officially became a state. During the next three years, all thirteen colonies became states. At the same time, the United States created the first official US territory.

Establishing territories allowed the **federal government** to manage the huge swaths of land claimed by the United States. These lands were the homelands of Native American tribes. The US government wrote peace treaties with individual tribes, granting them ownership of certain lands in exchange for peaceful relations with nearby settlers.

White men living in a US state paid taxes, had the right to vote, and had representation in the US Senate and House of Representatives. Those living in territories didn't pay taxes, had no government representation, and couldn't vote in presidential elections.

When territorial populations and their economies grew large enough, settlers petitioned the US Senate to let their territories become states. In proposing a new state, Denver's settlers were following methods used by settlers elsewhere.

Meanwhile, despite treaties, as pioneers settled on Native American land, they forced tribes to move away. Were Native Americans citizens? Could they vote? How was the United States able to break peace treaties?

3 Setting the Stage

When early Denver settlers began discussing statehood, the land that would eventually become the state of Colorado was actually part of four different US territories. The town of Boulder was in the Nebraska Territory. San Luis was in the New Mexico Territory. Breckenridge was in the Utah Territory. Denver City was in the Kansas Territory.

The capitals of the Nebraska, New Mexico, Utah, and Kansas Territories were far from the fledgling Rocky Mountain towns, leaving the remote Colorado communities isolated. There was no central government to impose law and order, so some communities formed **People's Courts.** Mining towns established **Miners' Courts.** These courts became legal authorities that recorded mining claims, certified property ownership, and addressed crime.

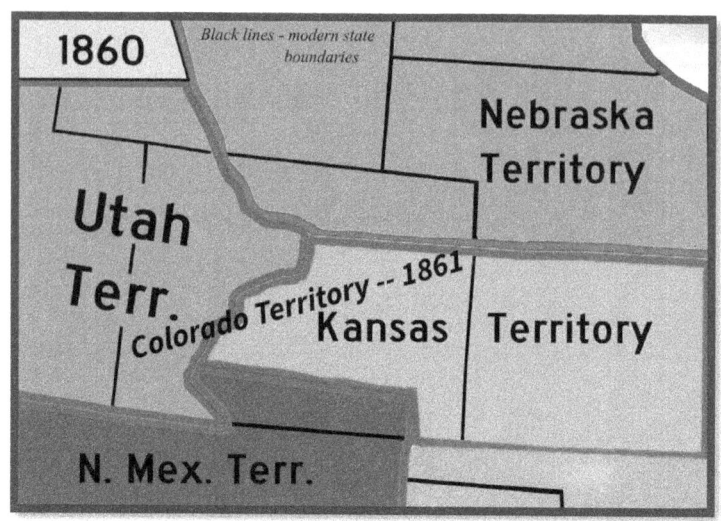

Colorado Territory was formed from land previously in the Kansas, Nebraska, Utah, and New Mexico Territories
Courtesy of Wikimedia

Crime was hard to manage. Some individuals accused of crimes were brought before a judge who had been selected from the men of the community. Sometimes the accused was tried in front of a jury, but sometimes settlers used **vigilante law**. In these cases, individuals took the law into their own hands and punished the accused without waiting for a trial.

The law was often hard to enforce. An article from August 1926, in *Colorado Magazine,* described attitudes toward government before the Colorado Territory was officially established:

Setting the Stage

The enactment of laws was easily accomplished, but the execution was quite another matter. . . . When a poll tax of one dollar was levied to defray [expenses of the temporary government] . . . six hundred miners from the mountain camps signed a "pledge to resist the collection of any tax imposed by the Provisional Government," and promised the collectors bullets instead of dollars.

Adding to the roadblocks of organizing Colorado into a new territory or state were the treaties signed by the US government and Native American tribes. Illinois senator Stephen Douglas, who challenged Abraham Lincoln in the 1860 presidential election, pointed out—on the floor of the US Senate—that even talking about Colorado statehood was absurd because the land the settlers and miners wanted for a state was owned by **sovereign** tribal nations.

It wasn't until 1864 that Congress, breaking Native American treaties, gave clear land titles to Colorado settlers and miners.

An 1958 US postage stamp commemorating the Lincoln and Douglas debates.

Know More
Who Were the First Coloradans?

Long before Colorado became a hot spot for gold seekers, the Colorado plains and mountains were home to many Native American tribes, including the Cheyenne, Arapaho, Ute, Apache, and Comanche people. The Ute people are recognized as Colorado's oldest Native American tribe. **Archaeologists** believe the Ute people arrived in the Rocky Mountains between 1,000 and 2,000 years ago, although the Ute origin story states that they always lived in the Colorado mountains.

The Ute people were nomadic, roaming between the Front Range of the Rockies into parts of Utah and from northern New Mexico through southern Wyoming. The 1849 Treaty of Abiquiú ordered the Ute people to stop "their roving and rambling ways." The 1851 Treaty of Fort Laramie forced Cheyenne and Arapaho people to allow road construction across their lands and safe passage for settlers. With each new treaty, Native American lands were significantly reduced in size.

With the Pikes Peak gold rush and the settlers who came with it, the pressure to limit Native American territory and even to move Native American tribes out of Colorado intensified. Today, the only Native American **reservations** in Colorado are the Southern Ute and Mountain Ute Reservations in southern Colorado.

Who do you think had the right to live on the land? What happened to the tribes that once called Colorado home?

4 1859 Auraria Convention

In 1859, Representative Alexander Stephens introduced a bill in Congress to create the territory of Jefferson, named after former president Thomas Jefferson. This was the first name used for what would eventually become the Colorado Territory. Debates about slavery and the brewing Civil War stalled the effort and the bill failed.

The defeat in Congress did not slow efforts to achieve statehood by those living in Colorado. On April 11, 1859, fifty delegates from communities in and around the Rocky Mountains met in Auraria (Denver today). These men, as reported in the April 23, 1859, *Rocky Mountain News*, felt "the necessity of forming some government that will be a means of procuring safety to the large emigration now flowing into this country." At the meeting, which was called the Preliminary Convention, delegates resolved to form a "new and independent

State of the Union."

A new state required both a name and defined borders. Claiming land from four western territories, the men decided:

> That the State contemplated shall embrace the following territory . . . its northern boundary commencing at 102d meridian of west **longitude** from Greenwich, Eng., with the 43d parallel of north **latitude**, and running west on the said parallel to its intersection with the 110th meridian of west longitude, thence south to the 37th parallel of north latitude, thence east on that parallel to the 102d meridian, and thence north of the beginning; and that the name thereof shall be the State of JEFFERSON.

Colorado's area today is smaller by about 40 percent than the area proposed above.

The proposed boundaries of the state or territory of Jefferson
Courtesy of Wikimedia

On May 7, 1859, *The Rocky Mountain News* reprinted an address from the Preliminary Convention:

> Government of some kind we must have, and the question narrows itself down to this point: Shall it be the government of the knife and the revolver, or shall we unite in forming herein our golden country . . . a new and independent State?

The organizers also formed a committee to draft a **constitution** and **bylaws**. The committee of statehood advocates consisted of Richard Sopris, the President of the Gregory Association of Miners; William Byers, the owner of the *Rocky Mountain News*; and Col. Henry Allen, the President of the first Territorial Council of the Territory of Jefferson.

On August 13, 1859, the "Constitution of the State of Jefferson" was printed on the front page of *The Rocky Mountain News*. But the men who had drafted the constitution mostly lived along the Front Range. Miners in the mountains and Hispanos in southern Colorado had little input in creating the constitution. Leaving these future Coloradans out was part of the reason the statehood vote failed weeks later.

First page of the August 18, 1859, *Rocky Mountain News*, showing the "Constitution of the State of Jefferson"

1859 Auraria Convention

On August 20, 1859, *The Rocky Mountain News* announced the upcoming statehood vote for either statehood or territorial status under the headline, "Voters Take Notice!" The article explained that a vote "For Constitution" was a vote for statehood and was considered "a full and complete negative to a Territorial Organization." A vote "For Territory" was a vote for the formation of a new territory and was considered "a full and complete negative to a State Constitution."

Vote results were announced a month later. The majority of voters chose territorial status. They rejected the state constitution by 2007 to 1649.

A new convention went to work creating a **provisional** government and constitution for the Jefferson Territory. The delegates also wrote a document called "The Organic Act of the Territory of Jefferson." The document's audience was not local voters, but instead the US Congress. Only the federal government could grant Colorado the right to form as a territory or a state.

On New Year's Day 1860, Samuel Beall, representative of the Jefferson General Assembly, requested that Congress create the territory of Jefferson. By summer, a troubled US Congress, heavy with worries about a looming Civil War, adjourned without granting the Jefferson Territory permission to organize.

The United States had other, bigger worries.

Know More
Why Would Colorado citizens Want to Become a Territory? Why a State?

- **Taxation**: A state could tax its citizens and use the money to fund courts, schools, and other organizations. A territory received federal funding and did not have taxes.
- **Land Ownership**: A state would send representatives to Congress to make decisions about land and mine ownership.
- **Self-Government**: Citizens of a state could elect their own government officials and establish courts and laws. In a territory, the governor was appointed by the US president, with no voice from citizens of the territory.
- **Representation:** Citizens of a state could vote in federal elections and have their own representation in Congress. Individuals in a territory did not have representation in Congress and could not even vote on their own governor.

How would you have voted? Why?

5

1860 to 1861
Civil War Stalls Statehood

Colorado settlers and miners would have to wait on their territorial or statehood status. The United States was on the verge of a civil war over the enslavement of Black Americans. Southern states allowed slavery, and northern states did not. **Abolitionists** wanted to ban slavery throughout the nation. **Compromises** about slavery had kept the country together for decades. The **Missouri Compromise of 1820** laid out a plan to keep the number of free states (states without slavery) and slave states (states that allowed slavery) equal in number.

The state of Jefferson, if allowed to enter the country, would be a free state and would upend that balance. Colorado's low population also played into the question of statehood.

The **1787 Northwest Ordinance,** which defined

how a territory or state would be created, said that a territory needed to have at least five thousand adult males living in it. The ordinance also specified that sixty thousand adult males were needed for a region to become a state.

The 1860 census set the Pikes Peak area population at 34,277. Too few to qualify as a state, but enough for a territory. But many of the men pushing for statehood said the area's population was higher than reported because a significant number of backcountry miners lived too remotely to be counted. Governor Robert Steele—elected by the provisional government in October 1859 but not recognized by the federal government—declared in the November 15, 1860, *Rocky Mountain News* that the census results showed "sixty thousand souls."

For the creation of either a territory or a state, the Northwest Ordinance required Congress to pass an **enabling act**. With this act, the settlers in the region had the right to write a territory or state constitution. The constitution would then need to be accepted by popular vote by the citizens of the region before Congress could pass a bill recommending the creation of a territory or a state.

Republican Party candidate Abraham Lincoln won the US presidential election in November 1860, becoming the first Republican president. Southern states feared that the Republicans would

1860 to 1861 Civil War Stalls Statehood

abolish slavery. They began considering **secession**. In February 1861, southern states began to secede from the United States, forming the Confederate States of America.

Despite the turmoil, Colorado's bid to become a territory was not dead. One of the last things President James Buchanan did before vacating his office to make way for President Lincoln was to sign an act creating the Colorado Territory. The new territory was approximately 41 percent smaller than the proposed Jefferson Territory, with borders that match current state borders. The organization of the Colorado Territory helped the United States gain control of the mineral-rich Rocky Mountains at a time when it desperately needed Colorado's gold and silver to help pay for military expenses.

Why was the name changed from Jefferson Territory to Colorado Territory? According to C. C. Bradford's 1918 textbook, *A War-Modified Course of Study for the Public Schools of Colorado*, several names were proposed for the territory including "Idaho, Montana, San Juan, Columbus, Lulu, Lafayette, and Jefferson." It was William Gilpin, President Lincoln's appointee as the first governor of the Colorado Territory, who proposed the name Colorado. The name means "colored red" in Spanish.

Colorado officially became a territory on February 28, 1861. On March 4 of the same year, Lincoln was sworn in as the sixteenth president. First territorial Governor Gilpin headed west to set up the territorial government just a month before Confederate troops fired on Fort Sumter, a federal fort in South Carolina's Charleston Harbor.

The Civil War had begun.

By June, eleven states had seceded from the Union. Many miners left the Colorado Territory to **enlist** in either the Confederate or the Union Army. This left Colorado's mines without enough miners just when the Union Army needed gold from Colorado's mines.

States that seceded from the Union during the Civil War
Courtesy of History on the NET

1860 to 1861 Civil War Stalls Statehood

For settlers who stayed in the Colorado Territory, participation in the Civil War was limited. But in March 1862, Colorado volunteers, fighting for the Union, met and repelled Texas cavalry troops under the command of Confederate Brigadier General Henry Sibley. The fight was called the Battle of Glorieta Pass. The battle boosted the Colorado Territory's Union allegiance.

Despite the turbulence of the Civil War, the business of organizing the territory of Colorado moved forward. A territorial convention gathered and **ratified** a constitution.

Colorado's position on rights of Black men became clear in October 1861. During its first session, the legislature of the Colorado Territory removed the word *white* from voting requirements in the territorial Constitution. As of winter 1861, all men twenty-one years old or older had the right to vote in the Colorado Territory.

That remarkable right, given the Civil War and the nation's long history with slavery, was short-lived. In March 1864, the territorial legislature again changed election laws, this time **disfranchising** Black men. Colorado's Black men had held the right to vote for only three years.

> ## Know More
> ## President Lincoln, Slavery, and Suffrage for Black Men
>
> Abraham Lincoln is best remembered for ending slavery through the 1863 **Emancipation Proclamation** and for saving the Union through the Civil War.
>
> In the 1850s, Lincoln's Republican Party emerged as the dominant voice against slavery in the United States. At that time, abolishing slavery was not at the center of Republican policy, but a group known as Southern Democrats saw the Republicans—and Lincoln—as a threat to slavery.
>
> During this period of political turmoil, the Colorado Territory's decision in 1861 to grant Black men the right to vote was a bold move. Why do you think Coloradans made this decision?
>
> Three years later, when the word *white* was again included in the voting requirements in the proposed state constitution, Black Americans were furious. Many of them had moved to the Colorado Territory because the territory had granted them the right to vote.
>
> Why do you think the men writing the proposed Colorado State constitution removed the right of Black men to vote three years after they had granted the right?

6
1862 to 1864 Turbulent Politics

While the Civil War raged, Colorado shaped its new territorial constitution and government. Due to financial issues, territorial Governor Gilpin was replaced by John Evans as the appointed governor. Evans would play a pivotal role in the territory's history because of the 1864 **Sand Creek Massacre**.

Hiram P. Bennet was selected as the territory's 1862 non-voting delegate to the US House of Representatives. According to an article in the fall 1976 *Colorado Magazine*, Bennet had "a strong background in politics and law." In March 1860, he used skillful **oratory** skills and his knowledge of law to save an accused murderer from being killed by an angry mob. He convinced the vigilantes that a trial in a People's court would be more "decent and becoming."

In the trial that followed, Bennet acted as the prosecuting attorney responsible for persuading the jury that the man was guilty. He was successful. The jury convicted the prisoner, and the murderer was hanged.

As a Colorado territorial delegate, Bennet could not vote in the House of Representatives, but he could use his considerable oratorical skills to influence his peers. On February 28, 1863, Bennet made a passionate plea for Colorado statehood on the House floor.

Article in the October 5, 1863, *Rocky Mountain News*, supporting Colorado's bid for statehood

He petitioned again in the fall of 1863. Finally on May 25, 1864, the US Congress voted on an **enabling act**. This legislation granted citizens of the territory of Colorado the right to create a state constitution as their first step toward seeking statehood. Colorado citizens would then vote on

1862 to 1864 Turbulent Politics

the proposed constitution. If a majority voted for the constitution, the territory could apply for statehood. Coloradans would still need the US Senate to vote them into the Union and for the US president to sign the statehood bill.

One reason Congress changed its mind about letting Colorado apply for statehood was the fear that President Lincoln would not be re-elected in 1864. Passing enabling acts for Colorado, Nevada, and Nebraska Territories was part of a strategy from the Republican Congress to add votes for Lincoln. All three territories leaned Republican and their admission as states would add nine more **electoral votes** and numerous voters who favored re-electing Lincoln.

On July 11, 1864, a new Colorado constitutional convention backed a state constitution that clearly declared that the new state would be against slavery. The constitution included the statement, "Slavery shall never exist, nor involuntary servitude, except for the punishment of crime, whereof the party shall have been duly convicted." Although the document denounced slavery, it also said that only white males could vote in Colorado.

Free Black men living in Colorado who had been voting for the previous three years were outraged. Colorado Hispano voters were also angry because they had been excluded from the convention that had drafted the new constitution. Women had no say at all. They were not allowed to vote until 1893.

When Colorado men voted on October 11, 1864, voters rejected the constitution by a vote of 1520 to 4672. The Hispano voice was clear. Hispano populations living in Costilla, Huerfano, and Conejos counties said no to the new state constitution by a vote of 1,285 to 125.

Colorado remained a territory. The Civil War began turning in the North's favor. President Lincoln won his second term without votes from any citizens of the western territory. If Colorado wanted to become a state, statehood proponents would have to change their strategy.

Know More
Colorado's Hispano Population

Congress chose the 37th parallel as the southern border for the Colorado Territory, including a corner of the New Mexico Territory. Living on this land in 1861 were approximately seven thousand Hispanos settlers.

The Hispano pioneers had settled in southern Colorado years before the Pikes Peak gold rush. They had established the first non-native towns, churches, and businesses in the region. After the Mexican-American War, Hispanos were granted full American citizenship, but Colorado pioneers often didn't recognize this. They experienced terrible prejudices, and often they were not granted the same rights that other American citizens enjoyed.

7 1865 Statehood Skeptics

Despite their 1864 defeat, Colorado leaders had not given up on becoming a state. Territorial governor John Evans, future territorial and state governor John Routt, and *Rocky Mountain News* owner William Byers led the call for statehood. To succeed, they would have to appeal to those who were wary of statehood.

They started with the mountain mining communities, arguing that statehood was in their best interest. For the most part, Colorado miners had consistently voted against statehood. They were struggling to survive and worried about higher taxes and other government fees.

Statehood advocates pointed out that as a state, Colorado would have full representation in Congress. Their congressional representatives could vote on US policy. Statehood would also allow Colorado citizens to vote in presidential elections and as a state, Colorado could receive federal funds for building roads, bridges, and other **infrastructure.**

The most important issue to Colorado miners was mining claim ownership. If Colorado were a state, miners could appeal to the US government through their congressional representatives to deny Native American rights to the land they had once occupied. Without any voting rights or representation in government, Native Americans would have little say in their future within the would-be state of Colorado.

Statehood advocates also pointed out that Colorado congressmen and senators could help make sure the transcontinental railroad ran through Colorado. If the railroad bypassed Colorado, it would be a long-term blow to the economy, and to mining.

This heated campaign for Colorado statehood came as America's Civil War seemed to be coming to an end. When Confederate General Robert E. Lee surrendered to Union General Ulysses S. Grant on April 9, 1865, at Appomattox Court House, the Civil War effectively ended. Just six days later, on April 15, 1865, assassin John Wilkes Booth killed President Abraham Lincoln at Ford's Theater in Washington, DC. Although Colorado was geographically distant from the war and Washington, these nation-changing events postponed the march to statehood.

1865 Statehood Skeptics

But they didn't silence it.

On July 11, 1865, T*he Weekly Mining Journal* in Black Hawk discussed the pros and cons of statehood in an article entitled "State or Territory?" In the article, the writer questioned if Colorado was ready for statehood using a bit of **satire**:

> Indeed, Miss Colorado must carefully consider whether it is advisable at the present time to become one of the many wives of that respectable old gentleman, Uncle Sam [the United States], and whether she can present as respectable an appearance as her mates [other states], or would be ridiculous from the paucity of her wardrobe [small economy and population].

After another Colorado state convention adopted a new state constitution, Coloradans were again asked to vote on statehood. On September 5, Coloradans voted yes to accept the constitution with a vote of 3,025 to 2,870, a majority of only 155 votes.

While miners had been wooed throughout the statehood process, Black men who had lost their right to vote, were offered only a chance at obtaining suffrage again. The 1865 statehood vote included a proposal to return Black male suffrage. White male Coloradans voted 4,192 to 476 against this basic right of citizenship.

Know More
Why was John Evans Forced to Resign?

On November 29, 1864, Colonel John M. Chivington led a force of 1st Colorado Infantry Regiment volunteers and 3rd Regiment Colorado Cavalry volunteers and massacred hundreds of friendly Cheyenne and Arapaho men, women, and children camped near Sand Creek. Several of the Cheyenne and Arapaho leaders who died in this massacre had met with both Chivington and Territorial Governor John Evans just months earlier. Although a peace treaty had not been negotiated then, the Native Americans were instructed to camp near Fort Lyon along Sand Creek until negotiations could be continued.

During the time of the massacre, Evans was both the Colorado territorial governor and the superintendent of Indian affairs. Although it is not believed that Evans help plan the attack, many felt he helped create the environment that made the massacre possible. Although both Evans and Chivington lost their political and military positions, no one involved in the massacre was punished for the killings.

Do you think Evans was treated fairly? Should Chivington have been punished for ordering the killing these Native Americans? Should soldiers have been punished for massacring Native Americans, including elderly people, women, and children, even though they were following an officer's orders?

1865   Statehood Skeptics

In October 1865, Alexander Cummings, the new Territorial Governor, arrived in Colorado. With the end of the war and voters' acceptance of the state constitution, statehood seemed certain—at least to Coloradans. Eugene H. Berwanger wrote in his book, *The Rise of the Centennial State: Colorado Territory, 1861-76*:

> The "state" legislature convened in December and proceeded to act as if the territorial government no longer existed. "Certain persons" contacted members of the territorial legislature and informed them that their scheduled meeting for January 1866 was unnecessary and they would not be paid if they did assemble.

Territorial governor Cummings reminded Coloradans that Colorado would remain a territory—and hence be governed by the territorial legislature—until the Senate and the president granted statehood.

From the start, Cummings had not been well liked by most Coloradans. He'd been appointed after the popular Governor John Evans had been forced to resign because of the Sand Creek Massacre, where Colorado troops killed hundreds of Native Americans. Cummings's support of federal law made it appear that he was against statehood.

Coloradans, believing they were on the cusp of

statehood, were ready to elect their own governor, not be ruled by a Washington appointee. Cummings's adversarial relationship with powerful Coloradans only worsened when he fought to reinstate the right of Black men to vote.

Colorado's Black leaders—encouraged by Cummings's support—presented Cummings with a petition signed by 137 Black Coloradan men detailing their struggle for suffrage. They asked that the petition be presented to the US Congress and requested that the Senate "not admit the Territory as a State until the word white be erased from her State Constitution."

When Cummings sent the petition to the Senate, the backlash against him was quick and harsh. Coloradans had written a state constitution and had accepted this constitution in a general election. They wanted statehood. Cummings—appointed by the US president, not elected by Coloradans—appeared to be trying to thwart their efforts. In April 1867, Cummings resigned his governorship.

1865 Statehood Skeptics

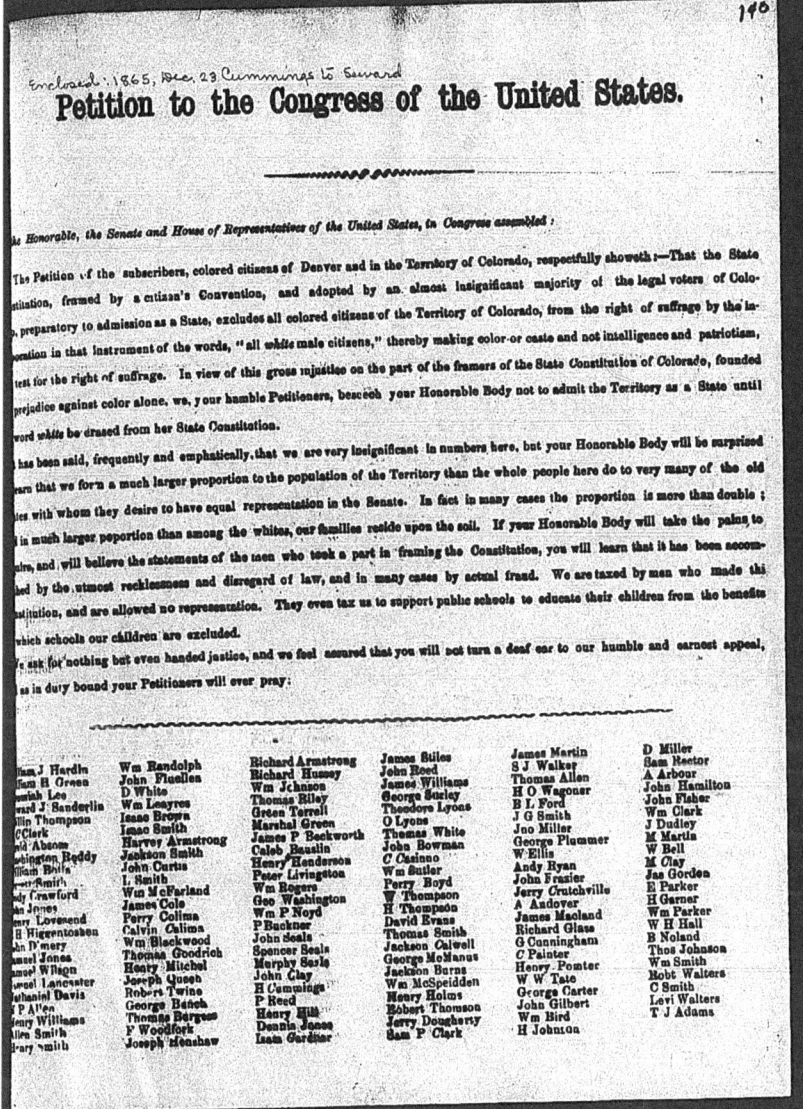

The 1865 petition sent to Congress by Colorado Black men asking for their right to vote
Courtesy of History of the National Archives

8 1866 and 1867 Vetoes

In March 1866, the US Senate took up the Colorado statehood bill. Although there were discussions about Black suffrage, most concerns focused on the Colorado Territory's low population. If Colorado became a state, it would lose its current federal funding, placing a financial hardship on its citizens. Senators felt the population was too small to take on those burdens and only a small majority of Congressmen supported statehood.

Senators rejected the bill.

But on March 27, 1866, President Andrew Johnson vetoed the Civil Rights Act, enraging Republicans in Congress. The Senate returned to the Colorado statehood bill—this time with the goal to obtain more Republican representatives in Congress to **override** the president. The statehood bill was approved on May 3, 1866.

Once again, jubilant pro-state Coloradans, certain of their statehood bid, celebrated. On May 4, 1866, just one day after the bill was approved, *The Rocky Mountain News* published an article titled "The State of Colorado." In this article, Allen Bradford, Colorado's territorial delegate to Congress, said "there is not the slightest danger of the president vetoing the bill." But, on January 28, 1867, President Johnson vetoed the bill.

Historians explain the president's veto in different ways. On the one hand, Johnson was worried that Colorado's population was too small for statehood. There would only be a single congressman from Colorado in the House, compared to thirty-one from New York. On the other hand, historians point to the political consequences Johnson would have faced if two more pro-Republican voices were added to the Republican majority in the Senate. This was especially important since confederate states had not yet been readmitted to the Union, so their representatives did not, at that time, have a voice in Congress.

Hoping to override the presidential veto, lawmakers introduced a new Colorado statehood bill later in 1867. To satisfy Radical Republicans (who insisted Black men should have the right to vote), the new bill included a provision that Colorado would be admitted as long as the word *white* was removed from the state constitution as a requirement for voting. This change would give suffrage to Black men. The bill passed both houses of Congress.

Again, President Johnson vetoed it.

Congress turned their attention to a new bill, the Territorial Suffrage Act, which would give Black men the right to vote in all territories. This bill passed on January 10, 1867, and although President Johnson did not sign it, he allowed the bill to become law without his signature. Black men in Colorado again had the right to vote in territorial elections, and now they threw in their support behind statehood.

Know More
How Does the President Veto a Bill?

The main job of the US Congress is to pass laws. If a president doesn't agree with a law that Congress has approved, he or she can veto it. This is an important component of the US government's checks and balances system. It prevents any of the three branches of government from becoming too powerful. Congress can override a presidential veto with a two-third majority vote in both the House of Representatives and the Senate, but such a vote is difficult to obtain.

Do you think a veto gives the president too much authority? Why do you think President Johnson kept vetoing the Colorado statehood bill?

9 1868 to 1875
Almost a State

In the late 1860s and early 1870s, Colorado's economy and population began to grow. New gold extraction methods using **smelters** instead of **stamp mills** increased mining production. New agricultural techniques increased crop output. Colorado became cattle country, especially when rancher Charles Goodnight brought cattle into Colorado along the Pecos Trail, establishing ranches near Trinidad and Pueblo.

Railroads caused the biggest boom in Colorado's population, economy, and prosperity. As the Civil War raged, Congress passed the Pacific Railway Act in 1862 and authorized the construction of the first **transcontinental** rail line.

Initial excitement in Colorado over the coming of a railway was followed by disappointment when the Union Pacific Railroad chose to bypass Denver and lay its line through Cheyenne in present-day Wyoming. Understanding the vital importance of a railroad terminal in Colorado,

Denverites formed the Denver Pacific Railroad and Telegraph Company. The Union Pacific Railroad agreed to install a spur line between Cheyenne and Denver if the Denver Pacific agreed to grade the roadbed and lay the ties.

Railroad politics caused most of that spur to be paid for by Coloradans, but the first train from Cheyenne rolled into Denver in June 1870. By the fall, the Colorado Territory was connected by rail to California, St. Louis, and Omaha.

Before the coming of the railroad, Colorado Territory's economy was driven by mining. After

Denver's railroad station, at the end of Twenty-Second Street
Courtesy of Denver Public Library, Z-169

1868 to 1875 Almost a State 41

the railroad arrived, farming, ranching, and other agricultural endeavors became an important part of the territory's economy.

The railroad also brought new settlers. After the arrival of the railroad, the Colorado Territory's population jumped from the 1870 census count of 39,864 to an estimated population of 80,000 in 1872. Also based on census counts, the region increased in population from 34,277 in 1860 to 194,327 in 1880. This number did not include Native Americans. They were not included in most census figures until the 1890s and did not gain citizenship or voting rights until 1924.

As the territory's population grew, the number of women in the territory increased, but the percent of women compared to men decreased. The 1860 census reported that only 4.6 percent of the regional population was female. This means that in a group of one hundred Coloradans, only four or five were women. The 1870 census showed that women made up 37.3 percent of the population, but by 1880, women made up just 27.3 percent, a drop of 10 percent. Harsh living conditions and limited economic opportunities for women contributed to this drop.

Some of Colorado's population gain came from **cooperative colonies.** In 1870, 144 families joined the Union Coloney, organized by Nathan Meeker, and formed the town of Greeley. The Chicago-Colorado Colony settled along the Denver Pacific Railroad route and formed the town of Longmont. Carl Wulsten helped establish the German Colonization Society which settled in the Wet Mountain Valley near Silver Cliff. Most of the colonies were short-lived, but many of the towns they formed survived.

As these communities became more established, many foreign immigrants became US citizens. These new citizens became yet another group that statehood advocates needed to attract.

Some of the population gain was attributed to the Colorado Territorial Board of **Immigration**. Organized by the territorial legislature in 1870, the board sent agents to eastern states and to Europe. The agents distributed seventy-seven thousand pamphlets that praised Colorado's beauty and farmland in an attempt try to attract new settlers to the territory.

The railroad made Colorado more attractive to settlers by giving easier access to basic goods from the East. Since goods were easier to come by, prices fell. In 1865, a sack of flour cost $25 in Colorado, but by 1875, that same sack cost only $2.50.

Know More
What Was the Dearfield Colony?

In 1910, Oliver Toussaint Jackson, inspired by the white colony at Greeley, established Dearfield, the largest Black homesteading settlement in Colorado. By 1915, there were forty-four cabins on **homestead** claims there. The agricultural products produced by the Black settlers made the settlement prosperous. During World War I, Dearfield had an estimated three hundred residents. The town had two churches, a concrete block manufacturer, a lumber and coal yard, a store, and a hotel. The 1930s Dust Bowl, when the topsoil dried out and blew away in the wind, forced most Dearfield homesteaders to leave to find work in nearby cities.

Do you think Dearfield was like other colonies in Colorado? Why or why not?

Dearfield settlers, circa 1920-1930
Courtesy of Denver Public Library, ARL58-2021-839

Images from a brochure printed by the Colorado Territorial Board of Immigration
Courtesy of the Library of Congress, Control Number tmp92001497

Colorado congressional territorial delegate Jerome B. Chaffee never gave up on statehood. During these years of growth, he consistently reminded Congress and President Ulysses S. Grant of the territory's increasing prosperity and population. The territory's population had swelled well above the sixty thousand people required for statehood. Finally, in 1873, President Ulysses S. Grant recommended passage of an enabling act for Colorado statehood.

10 1876 Statehood at Last

It took Congress two years, but on March 3, 1875, Coloradans celebrated when Congress passed legislation allowing Colorado to host a convention, and draft another state constitution, as they had done several times before. Now there was new optimism. During the next few months, newspapers across the territory bantered the pros and cons of statehood. *The Colorado Transcript* noted on March 24, 1875, that as a state, Colorado would assume "the responsibilities, perils, and advantages and increased financial burdens of Statehood."

Despite a few naysayers, Colorado organized a new, and its last, state convention on December 20, 1875. The delegates set to work to draft a new state constitution.

Confident statehood was coming, Colorado women, who had been fighting for the right to vote for years, renewed their efforts. In January 1876, women had a convention at the Unity Church of Denver. The Territorial Woman Suffrage Society was formed, and their representatives presented their case at the constitutional convention.

According to Joseph Brown's book *The History of Equal Suffrage in Colorado*, the men were "amused by the errand of the ladies." The proposed amendment for women's suffrage was defeated twenty-four to eight, although the right of women to vote in school board elections, which had been part of the territorial constitution, was included in the new state constitution.

Ultimately, language about future decisions on women's suffrage did make it into the state constitution. Article 7, Section 2 of the constitution stated:

> The General Assembly shall, at the first session thereof, and may at any subsequent session, enact laws to extend the right of suffrage to women of lawful age, and otherwise qualified, according to the provisions of this Article. No such enactment shall be of effect until submitted to the vote of the qualified electors at a general election, nor unless the same be approved by a majority of those voting thereon.

An amendment to the US Constitution requires a positive vote from two-thirds of the delegates in the Senate and House. However, because of the language in Colorado's state constitution required only a majority vote by the state's male voters, women won their right to vote on November 7, 1893. At that time, male Coloradans voted 35,798

Know More
Albina Votes in a School Board Election

Albina Washburn, an early Colorado pioneer who spent her life fighting for women's rights, decided she would vote in a school board election. She had her husband list her as the owner of several ponies, and she paid the taxes on them. As a tax-paying citizen over the age of twenty-one, she showed up to vote at her local school board election. In 1874, she voted without anyone's objection, but the next year she was stopped and told that a woman was not a citizen and therefore could not vote.

Albina consulted *Webster's Dictionary* and pointed out that citizen was defined as a person of either sex. The objectors relented, and Albina was permitted to vote. Even so, throughout their fight for suffrage, women were often accused of being as non-citizens.

What would you do if you were told you couldn't vote? Should women have used their influence in their families and communities to block statehood until they were guaranteed suffrage?

A Colorado woman fights for her right
of citizenship, circa 1915
Courtesy of Denver Public Library, X-29646

to 59,551—just under a 55 percent majority—to allow women's suffrage. Colorado women had won the right to vote twenty-seven years before the United States ratified the Nineteenth Amendment, which gave US women the right to vote.

In the spring of 1876, Colorado's state constitution was completed. It was approved by voters on July 1, 1876, by a vote of 15,443 to 4,052. On August

1, 1876, President Grant signed the bill that, after years of efforts, gave Colorado statehood.

In August 1926, Henry J. Hersey, a former judge of the District Court of Denver, wrote in *Colorado Magazine*:

> Colorado's admission to the Union is not alone significant because it occurred 100 years after the Declaration of Independence, but also because the efforts for governmental independence were accompanied by heroic and almost revolutionary (though peaceful) acts.

Know More
What Would You Have Done?

Colorado citizens tried for seventeen years—from 1859 to 1876—to create a state. During those years Oregon, Kansas, West Virginia, Nevada, and Nebraska were admitted as states. Which of the challenges to statehood do you think most affected Colorado's admission as a state? Why do you think Henry J. Hersey thought Colorado's admission to the Union was "accompanied by heroic and almost revolutionary . . . acts"?

How would you go about fighting for statehood? Or would you? The next states to be admitted after Colorado were North and South Dakota, Montana, and Washington, all in 1889. Why do you think it took thirteen years to admit more states?

11 The Centennial State

Colorado became the thirty-eighth state in the Union on August 1, 1876, four weeks after the United States celebrated its centennial birthday. In 1876, Colorado newspapers reported on the celebrations of the state's status as the centennial state in numerous ways. The Denver & Rio Grande Railway renamed its route through the Arkansas Valley the Centennial Route. The July 8, 1876, *Colorado Miner* reported that Georgetown celebrated with a "handsome flag with a golden star in the center, surrounded by the legend, 'Centennial State, 38.'" Colorado's Centennial State exhibit at the 1876 World's Fair in Philadelphia featured Martha Maxwell's **taxidermy** display of Colorado wildlife.

The Centennial State

The Colorado Centennial State exhibit at the 1876 World's Fair in Philadelphia featuring the work of Martha Maxwell
Courtesy of the Library Company of Philadelphia, Centennial Photographic Co., photographer

To accommodate its diverse population, the Colorado State Constitution was written in English and translated into Spanish and German. The Spanish version was for the state's large Hispano population in southern Colorado, and the German version was for Colorado's many German immigrants. Germans made up Colorado's largest foreign-born population at that time.

The cover of the 1876 Colorado State Constitution (above), which was also printed in Spanish and German (below)
Courtesy of History Colorado, MSS716.b.1 (English), 3509001 (Spanish), and 30001369 (German)

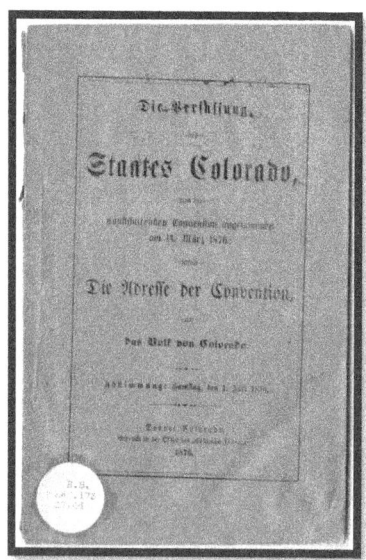

These last steps—including immigrants and the Hispano residents in Southern Colorado, along with creating a pathway for women to claim full citizenship rights in their state—all played a role in Colorado becoming the Centennial State. They were just as important as the discovery of gold in the Rocky Mountains, when the first seeds of statehood had been planted.

While the statehood campaign succeeded when it became more inclusive, its success still rested on the loss of Native American tribal lands. When Colorado achieved statehood in 1876, most Arapaho, Cheyenne, and other Native American tribes had been removed from Colorado's eastern plains.

An 1876 American flag with the thirty-eighth star representing the new state of Colorado
Courtesy of the River Junction Trade Co., RiverJunction.com

By 1880, the Utes had lost most of their mountain homeland to the United States.

Colorado's state land came from Native American tribal homelands. Its name came from the Spanish word meaning "colored red," after the rich red clay beneath Coloradans' feet. It is a prosperous land of unbelievable beauty with a fascinating history.

Timeline

1859—Fifty delegates frame a state constitution, which was submitted to a popular vote.

1860—Samuel Beall, at the behest of the Jefferson General Assembly, asks the US Congress to form the territory of Jefferson.

1860—The 1860 census counts the population of the Pike's Peak region at 34,277.

1861—Congress passes the Colorado Organic Act, creating the territory of Colorado. President James Buchanan signs the bill, establishing the Colorado Territory on **February 28, 1861**.

1861—**March 25**, William Gilpin is appointed by Abraham Lincoln as Colorado's first Territorial Governor.

1861—**October 18**, In the first session of the Colorado legislature, the word *white* is struck from the territorial constitution, giving Black males the right to vote.

1862—**March 26**, Territorial governor William Gilpin is replaced by John Evans.

1862—The territorial population declines as men head east to both the North and the South to fight in the Civil War.

1862—**July 1,** The Pacific Railway Act is signed into law, starting the development of the transcontinental railroad.

1863—January 1, President Abraham Lincoln issues the Emancipation Proclamation.

1863—Territorial delegate Hiram P. Bennet petitions the US House of Representatives for Colorado statehood

1864—March 11, The Colorado territorial legislature amends election laws, disenfranchising Black males.

1864—March 21, Congress passes an enabling act for Colorado's admission as a state if its citizens write a constitution and accept it by popular vote.

1864—The new Colorado constitution, which disenfranchises Black men, is voted on and rejected because of fears of high taxes and men being drafted into the US military.

1864—November 29, Infantry and cavalry troops led by Colonel John M. Chivington massacre friendly Cheyenne and Arapaho people camped near Sand Creek.

1865—January 7 to February 2, Southern Cheyenne, Arapaho, and Sioux people join forces and attack thirty-five ranches, farms, and stagecoach stations in the South Platte River Valley in retaliation for the Sand Creek Massacre.

1865—April 9, Confederate general Robert E. Lee surrenders, effectively ending the Civil War.

1865—April 14, President Lincoln is assassinated.

1865—August 20, President Andrew Johnson formally declares the Civil War over.

1865—October 17, Alexander Cummings replaces

Timeline

John Evans as territorial governor.

1865 — September 5, A new state constitution is drafted and adopted by a small majority of 155 votes.

1865 — President Johnson vetoes Colorado's admission to the Union as a state.

1866 — March 27, President Johnson vetoes the Civil Rights Bill.

1866 — May 3, Congress passes another enabling act for Colorado's admission. President Johnson vetoes it on **January 28, 1867**.

1867 — April 21, Colorado territorial governor Alexander Cummings resigns.

1867 — March George Chilcott is declared Colorado's new territorial governor but never takes office.

1867 — May 8, Alexander Cameron Hunt replaces Chilcott as territorial governor.

1869 — April 17, Edward M. McCook replaces Hunt as territorial governor.

1870 — The first train arrives in Denver

1873, April 17, Samuel Hitt Elbert replaces McCook as territorial governor.

1874, July 26, Edward M. McCook replaces Elbert as territorial governor, serving his second term.

1875, February 8, John Long Routt replaces McCook as territorial governor. He is later elected Colorado's first state governor.

1875 — March 3, Congress passes an enabling act for Colorado and President Grant approves it.

1875 — December 20, A constitutional convention

begins drafting a new state constitution.

1876—February 15, Colorado constitutional convention delegates vote twenty-four to eight against women's suffrage.

1876—March 14, The Colorado constitutional convention adopts a new constitution.

1876—July 1, the Colorado Constitution was approved by Colorado citizens in a vote of three to one in favor.

1876—August 1, President Ulysses S. Grant issues a proclamation making Colorado the thirty-eighth state in the United States. It is nicknamed the Centennial State.

1893—November 7, Colorado women receive the right to vote.

New Words and Terms

Abolitionist: a member of the movement that believed slavery should not be allowed
Archaeologist: people who study human history
Bylaws: rules adopted by an organization or government for the management of day-to-day business
Centennial: a one hundredth anniversary
Citizen: a legal resident of a nation or state
Civil War: a conflict between the United States and the Confederate States of America, fought between 1861 to 1865
Congress: the legislative branch of the US government, consisting of the House of Representatives and the Senate
Confederacy: the Confederate States of America composed of eleven southern states that left the United States to fight to preserve slavery. The Confederacy was defeated in the Civil War.
Constitution: a document spelling out how a state or other organization will be governed
Compromise: an agreement in which each side makes concessions, accepting some terms they didn't like
Cooperative colonies: settlers who joined together voluntarily and helped each other economically, socially, and culturally through jointly owned

enterprises

Disenfranchise: deprive a person or a group of people of the right to vote

Economic downturn: a decline in the economy, often called a recession

Electoral votes: a vote in the electoral college, which casts votes for the US president and vice president on the behalf of states

Emancipation Proclamation: an 1863 presidential order declaring that all enslaved people within the states at war with the Union were free

Enabling act: legislation that allows a group to take a certain action, such as seeking to become a US state

Expedition: a journey organized and undertaken for a specific purpose often to an unknown area

Explorer: a person who travels around an unfamiliar area

Federal government: the central US government, based in Washington, D.C.

Fort Atkinson Treaty of 1853: a treaty with the Apache, Comanche, and Kiowa tribes. One reason for the treaty was to make passage along the Santa Fe Trail safer for settlers.

Fort Laramie Treaty of 1851: a treaty with the plains tribes. This treaty helped allow settlers to safely travel across Native American lands.

Front Range: a region in Colorado along the eastern foothills of the Rocky Mountains

Hispano: a person descended from Spanish settlers in the southwestern US

Homestead: a piece of US public land granted to a

New Words and Terms

settler. The settler had to live on and improve (farm) the land for five years before filing for ownership.

Immigration: people who move to a new country to live

Indigenous people: people inhabiting land or a geographical region from the earliest times

Infrastructure: organizational structures and public works like roads, power systems, and sanitation systems

Latitude: lines that measure north–south position on a map. The equator is at 0 degrees, the North Pole is at 90 degrees north, and the South Pole is at 90 degrees south. Lines of latitude are all parallel to each other.

Lobbying: trying to influence lawmakers to vote a certain way

Longitude: the distance east or west of an imaginary line running through Greenwich, England. Longitude is measured in degrees and minutes.

Miners' courts: part of early Colorado's justice system. Miners' courts mostly operated in mining camps and primarily dealt with mining claim disputes.

Missouri Compromise of 1820: a law that admitted Maine and Missouri as states to maintain a balance between slave and free states

Northwest Ordinance: a law passed in 1787 defining government for the Northwest Territory and setting out the procedures for admitting new states to the Union

Oratory: the art or practice of public speaking

Override: to reject or cancel a decision

Peace treaty: an agreement between two hostile parties to end a war or to define rules so they can work together

People's courts: part of early Colorado's justice system. People's courts were primarily in larger settlements and mostly dealt with crime.

Pikes Peak gold rush: the arrival of many people hoping to find gold in Colorado in 1859-1860

Placer gold: gold particles found in stream beds

Plains Indians: Various North American Indigenous peoples who inhabited the Great Plains prior to the arrival of settlers from the East

Population: the number of people living in a country or region

Proclamation: a formal public announcement

Provisional: temporary

Prospect: to search for mineral deposits such as silver and gold

Ratify: to make an official document legal

Reservations: areas of land in the United States set aside for Native Americans. In the 1800s, Native American tribes were often forced to live on reservations.

Satire: making something look or sound ridiculous to embarrass someone

Secession: to separate from a nation or state and become independent

Slavery: the practice of owning another person

Smelter: a furnace used to extract valuable metals

Sovereign: self-governing

New Words and Terms

Stamp mill: a device that crushes ore into smaller pieces to remove valuable metals

Suffrage: the right to vote in elections

Taxidermy: the art of stuffing and mounting the skins of birds, reptiles, and other animals for display

Territory: a geographical area with an organized government and an appointed governor. Or an area or region that is home to a group of people.

Transcontinental: something that spans an entire continent

Union: another name for the United States. The states that stayed loyal to the US government during the Civil War

Vigilante law: law enforcement without going through a legal process

Sources

Books and Reports

Berwanger, Eugene H. *The Rise of the Centennial State: Colorado Territory, 1861-76*. Chicago, IL: University of Illinois Press, 2007.

Blackhawk, Ned, Loretta Fowler, Peter Hayes, Frederick E. Hoxie, Andrew Koppelman, Carl Smith, Elliott West, and Laurie Zoloth. *Report of the John Evans Study Committee*. Evanston, IL: Northwestern University, 2014.

Bradford, Mary C. C. and Co-operating Educators. *A War-Modified Course of Study for the Public Schools of Colorado*. Denver, Department of Public Instruction, 1819.

Bromwell, Henrietta E., compiler. *Fiftyniners' Directory: Colorado Argonauts of 1858-1859*. Denver, 1926.

Brown, Joseph G. *The History of Equal Suffrage in Colorado 1868-1898*. Denver, News Job Printing Co., 1898.

Everett, Derek R. *Creating the American West: Boundaries and Borderlands*. Norman, University of Oklahoma Press, 2014.

Hafen, LeRoy R. and James H. Baker. *History of Colorado*. Denver, Linderman, 1927.

Magazines and Newspapers

Colorado Historic Newspapers Collection, Colorado

Sources

State Library, coloradohistoricnewspapers.org.

"A Gala Day in the Silver Queen." *Colorado Miner*, July 8, 1876.

"Constitution of the State of Colorado Adopted in Convention July 11, 1864." *Rocky Mountain News*, July 14, 1864.

"Constitution of the State of Jefferson." *Rocky Mountain News*, August 13, 1859.

"Election Returns." *Rocky Mountain News*, September 17, 1859.

"Outward Bound." *Colorado Transcript*, March 24, 1875.

"State Constitution." *Rocky Mountain News*, August 16, 1865.

"State or Territory?" *Weekly Mining Journal*, July 11, 1865.

"Voters Take Notice!" *Rocky Mountain News*, August 20, 1859.

Hafen, L. R. "Steps to Statehood in Colorado." *Colorado Magazine*, August 1926.

Hersey, Henry J. "The Colorado Constitution." *Colorado Magazine*, August 1926.

Kopel, David. "Colorado's Early Self-Government and Path to Statehood." *Reason*, August 1, 2018.

Noel, Thomas J. "All Hail the Denver Pacific: Denver's First Railroad." *Colorado Magazine*, Spring 1973.

Romero, Tom I. "Wringing Rights Out of the Mountains: Colorado's Centennial Constitution and the Ambivalent Promise of Human Rights and Social Equality." *Albany Law Review 69* (2006).

Silverman, Jason H. "Making Brick Out of Straw: Delegate Hiram P. Bennet." *Colorado Magazine*, Fall 1976.

Simms, Erika. "Colorado's Statehood Journey Was a Long Strange Trip." *Colorado Culture Magazine*, October 30, 2024.

Web Material

Athearn, Fredric J. "Land of Contrast: A History of Southeast Colorado." Bureau of Land Management—Colorado, 1985.
  https://www.nps.gov/parkhistory/online_books/blm/co/17/index.htm

Bureau of Immigration and Statistics. *The Natural Resources and Industrial Development and Condition of Colorado*. Denver: Bureau of Immigration and Statistics, 1889.
  https://www.loc.gov/item/tmp92001497/.

Colorado Encyclopedia. "History Colorado." ColoradoEncyclopedia.org.

Colorado State Archives.
  "The Constitution of the State of Colorado, Adopted in Convention, March 14, 1876." https://archives.colorado.gov/sites/archives/files/Colorado%20Constitution.pdf.

Daley, John. "Long Before Denver was here, nearly 50 Native American Tribes called the Front Range Home." Colorado Public Radio, April 3, 2023.
  https://www.cpr.org/2023/04/03/which-native-american-tribes-called-colorado-front-range-

Sources

home/.

Haggit, Craig. "Is Colorado a Square State?" Denver Public Library Special Collections and Archives, August 1, 2016. https://history.denverlibrary.org/new/western-history/colorado-square-state.

History on the Net. "Confederate States of America and the Legal Right To Secede." https://www.historyonthenet.com/confederate-states-america-2.

Hoopers, Lydia. "11 Things You Didn't Know About Colorado's Path to Statehood." *History Colorado*, July 20, 2018. https://www.historycolorado.org/story/seasonal/2018/07/20/11-things-you-didnt-know-about-colorados-path-statehood.

National Park Service. "Fort Laramie Treaty of 1851" (Horse Creek Treaty). https://www.nps.gov/articles/000/horse-creek-treaty.htm.

National Park Service. "Sand Creek Massacre: History & Culture."

Trembath, Brian. "Jefferson Territory: The Renegade State that Almost Replaced Colorado." Denver Public Library Special Collections and Archives, June 24, 2020. https://history.denverlibrary.org/news/literary-research/jefferson-territory-renegade-state-almost-replaced-colorado.

US Department of the Interior, Bureau Land Management. "General Land Office Records." https://glorecords.blm.gov.

Acknowledgments

Barbara would like to thank her editor, Julie VanLaanen, from Filter Press, for working with her and helping her fact-check this manuscript. Barbara would also like to extend her thanks to Doris Baker from Filter Press and Craig Haggit from the Denver Public Library. Both Doris and Craig provided invaluable feedback and critique on her manuscript. Finally, she would like to thank Katherine Mercier, the exhibit developer and historian who developed History Colorado's statehood exhibit. Katherine shared with Barbara her extensive knowledge about Colorado's fascinating history during its twisted road to statehood and helped critique the manuscript.

About the Author

A grandfather who relished talking about (and burying) his silver coin collection—taught Barbara Taylor how to spot a great story. More than a decade as a newspaper reporter in Wisconsin, Iowa, Illinois and Colorado honed her love of true tales. Students in her high school history classroom at Pomona High School, taught Barbara daily what matters to our country's collective memory. A new adventure with sixth- and seventh-graders at Evergreen Middle School drew her to the tall order of finding the essential excitement and elegance of the Colorado statehood story.

Barbara was named the Colorado History Teacher of the Year in 2020 by the Gilder-Lehrman Institute on the heels of winning the James Madison Memorial Fellowship in American History in 2019. Her work with the American Exchange Project, which sends US students to an American town very different from their own for one week, has given her tangible hope that young people—even when they disagree about important issues—are capable stewards of democracy.

Barbara has raised two lawyers, Carter and Glenna, and has embraced attorney daughter-in-law Carol, all of whom work to represent those who don't have loud enough voices to speak for themselves. Barbara is an enormous fan of her granddaughter, Lily.

Index

1787 Northwest Ordinance, 19, 20, 61
1849 Treaty of Abiquiú, 12
Allen, Henry, 15
Beall, Samuel, 17, 55
Bennet, Hiram P., 25, 56, 66
Booth, John Wilkes, 30
Byers, William, 15, 29
Chaffee, Jerome B., 44
Colorado Magazine, 10, 25, 49, 65, 66
Colorado Miner, 50, 65
Colorado Territorial Board of Immigration, 42, 44
Colorado Territory, 10, 13, 21-24, 26, 28, 33, 36, 40, 41, 55, 64, 66
Cummings, Alexander, Colorado Territorial Governor, 33, 34, , 56 57
Dearfield Colony, 43
Denver Pacific Railroad and Telegraph Company, 40, 42
Douglas, Stephen, 11
Emancipation Proclamation, 24, 56, 60
Evans, John, Colorado Territorial Governor, 25, 29, 32, 33, 55, 57, 64
Fort Atkinson Treaty of 1853, 6, 60
Fort Laramie Treaty of 1851, 6, 12, 60, 67
Gilpin, William, first Colorado Territorial Governor, 21, 22, 24, 55
Goodnight, Charles, 39
Grant, Ulysses S., 2, 30, 44, 49, 57, 58
Gregory, John, 6
House, Ernest Jr., 6
Jackson, George, 6
Jackson, Oliver Toussaint, 43
Jefferson Territory, 13, 14, 17, 19-21, 55, 67
Johnson, Andrew, US President, 36-38, 56, 57
Kansas Territory, 9, 10
Lincoln, Abraham, US President, 11, 20, 21, 24, 27, 28, 30, 55, 56
Maxwell, Martha, 50, 51
Meeker, Nathan, 41
Miners' Court, 9, 61

Index

Missouri Compromise of 1820, 19, 61
Nebraska Territory, 9, 10, 27
New Mexico Territory, 9, 10, 28
Nineteenth Amendment, 48
People's Court, 9, 26, 62
Pike, Zebulon, explorer, 3, 4
Pikes Peak gold rush, 1, 5, 6, 12, 28, 62
Preliminary Convention, 13, 15
Purcell, James, 4
Rocky Mountain News, 1, 13, 15-17, 20, 26, 29, 37, 65
Routt, John, 29, 57
Sand Creek Massacre, 25, 32, 33, 56, 67
Sibley, Henry, 23

Sopris, Richard, 15
State of Jefferson, 14-16, 19, 65
Steele, Robert, Jefferson Territory Governor, 20
Stephens, Alexander, US Representative, 13
Territorial Suffrage Act, 38
Territory of Colorado: See Colorado Territory
Territory of Jefferson: See Jefferson Territory
The Colorado Transcript, 45, 65
The Weekly Mining Journal, 31, 65
Union Pacific Railroad, 39, 40
Utah Territory, 9, 10
Washburn, Albina, 47
Wootton, Dick, 1
Wulsten, Carl, 42

More
Now You Know Books

The 1896 Leadville
Ice Palace
ISBN: 978-0-86541-266-8

Elizabeth Byers:
Denver Pioneer
ISBN: 978-0-86541-256-9

Chipeta:
Ute Peacemaker
ISBN: 978-0-86541-091-6

Elrey Jeppesen:
Aviation Pioneer
ISBN: 978-0-86541-259-0

Enos Mills:
Rocky Mountain
Naturalist
ISBN: 978-0-86541-072-5

Florence Sabin:
Teacher, Scientist,
Humanitarian
ISBN: 978-0-86541-139-5

General William Palmer:
Railroad Pioneer
ISBN: 978-0-86541-092-3

John Denver:
Man for the World
ISBN: 978-0-86541-088-6

John Wesley Powell:
Soldier, Explorer, Scientist
ISBN: 978-0-86541-080-0

www.ingramcontent.com/pod-product-compliance
Lightning Source LLC
Chambersburg PA
CBHW062103290426
44110CB00022B/2701